Dealing with the

Death of a Child

Marilyn L. Price

Dealing with the

Death of a Child

Marilyn L. Price

HONOR ✦ NET
PUBLISHERS

SAPULPA, OK

Dealing with the Death of a Child
ISBN 978-1-938021-47-3
Copyright © 2018 by Marilyn L. Price

Marilyn L. Price
P. O. Box 1584
Broken Arrow, OK 74013-1584

Published by HonorNet Publishers

HONOR✠NET
PUBLISHERS

P. O. Box 910
Sapulpa, OK 74067
Website: honornet.net

Acknowledgments

WILL ALWAYS BE GRATEFUL to God for the twelve years and two months I had with my little champion, my son Jerry Paul. I learned lessons from him that you'll not find in any textbook. The "real meaning" of life was exemplified through his life.

Initially at birth, his outward appearance was marred because he was born with a bilateral cleft of both the lip and palate. Through numerous surgical procedures and the wisdom and expertise of medical professionals over the twelve years of Jerry's life, his outward appearance was restructured. His inward character was intact all along—love, sensitivity, wisdom, mischief at times, and compassion—and was consistently revealed in his countenance and in his words and actions.

My son met his death while on a family vacation in
Estes Park, Colorado, July 3, 1969.

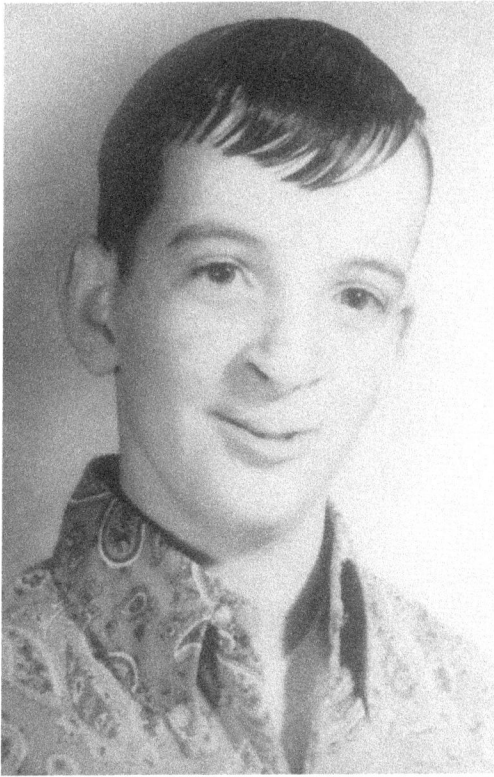

My champion, Jerry Paul

Contents

My Journey Following the Premature Death of My Son

F AR TOO OFTEN, I think we wait until someone dies physically—regardless of their age—to celebrate their life. Yet there are things we can do every day to celebrate others and encourage and edify them, not just on special occasions or at their homegoing. I have found that as you lift and encourage others, you will be lifted and encouraged yourself.

Since my firstborn, a precious son, was born with a bilateral cleft of the lip and palate, I was thrown into a new world which I knew little about. Today we would call my son a child with special needs since he had no ability to suck to receive nutrition to live. I learned quickly how to feed him by dropping formula into his mouth very slowly from a syringe.

In regard to premature death, the primary topic of this book, God is not in the business of taking babies, children, teenagers, or even adults before they have lived out their God-ordained and God-designed destinies. Simply put, God is not the author of tragedies, calamities, sickness and disease, or destruction of any kind at any age.

Neither is God the author of physical disabilities, for James 1:17 says, **"Every good gift and every perfect gift is from above, and comes down from the Father of lights, with whom there is no variation or shadow of turning."** Obviously, disabilities are not "good" or "perfect" gifts, yet God empowered me through His Holy Spirit to love, cherish, and make life as normal as possible for my son.

I have noticed that children who have a disability in one area often are exceptionally strong and even gifted in other areas. They desire to be loved and cherished as any other child. In fact, I have found that most children who have special needs are especially loving, sensitive, and readily receptive to the love and acceptance of others.

Psalm 127:3 says, **"Behold, children are a heritage from the Lord, the fruit of the womb is a reward."** *The New Living Translation* says, **"Children are a gift from the Lord; they are a reward from him."**

My son was a gift to me, just as my other children are. Life had some additional challenges because of his physical disability, but with God's help, with wonderful doctors and medical professionals, and with Jerry's "up" attitude, we walked through each one victoriously, although it was not an easy journey.

Jerry's medical challenges finally seemed to level off when he hit his twelfth birthday. Major surgeries were over and life took on what seemed to be some "upbeat" changes for my children and me. It was at this point, five weeks after I remarried, that Jerry died after falling while mountain climbing (going farther than he and his stepbrother were to go) without proper safety equipment or adult supervision.

I certainly do <u>not</u> have all the answers for premature death or for physical disabilities, but I can guarantee you, God is <u>not</u> the culprit! John 10:10 clearly identifies the job descriptions of both the devil and Jesus: "**The thief** [the devil] **does not come except to steal, and to kill, and to destroy. I** [Jesus Christ] **have come that they may have life, and that they may have it more abundantly.**"

The cause of tragedies and devastation in some cases can be traced to human error.

If you have experienced the premature death of a loved one or if you are dealing with a child with special needs, it is my heartfelt prayer that you will find comfort, healing, and encouragement and that you will laugh, love, and live again on a higher level after reading *Dealing with the Death of a Child*.

Marilyn L. Price

CHAPTER 1

Struck Down in the Rocky Mountains

THE SETTING: VACATIONING AS a family near Estes Park, Colorado, with other Air Guard families from my husband's workplace. On the sixth day of vacation, my husband, girls, and I headed into Estes Park to do laundry. My husband gave the boys permission to walk to a nearby mountain area while we went to do the laundry.

Other adults in our group were taking this particular day to hike in some of the nearby mountains. Our boys wanted to go with them, but obviously no one wanted the responsibility for watching over them. They wanted to truly enjoy the hike without added responsibility. Makes sense!

When we returned from doing the laundry, we were immediately met by a Park Ranger who asked, "Are you the Prices?" Answering in the affirmative, the Ranger said, "Follow me. One of your boys has fallen."

Life took a nasty turn that day. My husband and I had been married only five weeks. We were introduced by our pastor in whom I placed total trust because of the near-death experience that ended my first marriage. My husband's previous wife had died of cancer. I had two children, and my husband had two children.

Jerry, my son, had overcome every "mountain of physical challenge" he ever faced. He was a little champion—simply because his attitude was always "up" and on the "win" gauge regardless of what was going on in the natural. He was a fighter, never a quitter—and he loved life and filled it with joy!

At the direction of the Ranger, we drove to the foot of the mountain where our boys had walked while we went into town to do laundry. My husband's son was with the Rangers, so obviously it was my son who had fallen.

It took three hours for the Rangers to find Jerry while we waited at the base of the mountain. Numb and anxious, my primary prayer was, "Lord, please don't let there be any brain damage." Once Jerry was located, a medical doctor climbed the mountain to come to his aid.

Our car was turned so we could follow the ambulance into Boulder, but suddenly we were told to go to the nearby Medical Clinic. Within minutes the doctor walked in and said, "Your son was a fighter. I resuscitated him three times, but he is dead."

The autopsy report indicated that Jerry fell between 150 to 200 feet to his death.

End of story as far as Jerry's life on earth, but beginning of new life with Jesus in heaven for him. The beginning of grief and trauma for me as I had never dealt with the death of someone close to me nor had I been taught the truth about physical death of a born-again believer from God's perspective—from His Word.

I was born again and loved God with all of my heart, but I did not understand death or know how to deal with it. I was broken and grief-stricken, and I felt like a huge hunk of my heart had been ripped out of me.

We, along with the other Air Guard families who were with us, drove back to our homes in Iowa in a caravan, and Jerry's body was flown back to our hometown after an autopsy was performed in Colorado.

CHAPTER 2

"I'm Okay, Mom!"

DURING OUR two-day TRIP back to our homes in Iowa, suddenly I smelled the fragrance of roses so strong. At that moment we were driving through the barren fields of Nebraska, and I mean barren. There wasn't any grass where we were traveling, let alone any flowers or roses!

The fragrance was strong. Then, I heard Jerry in his own voice say, "I'm okay, Mom!" The fragrance momentarily subsided, then it came a second time every bit as strong, and again I heard Jerry's voice, "I'm okay, Mom!" My heart was still torn and broken, but this divine encounter brought comfort to me—even more in the days ahead than at that moment.

John 10:10 in the *New Living Translation* says, "**The thief's** [Satan's] **purpose is to steal and kill and destroy. My purpose** [Jesus' purpose] **is to give them a rich and satisfying life.**" Premature death doesn't contribute to a "**rich and satisfying life.**" Instead, I found that in the natural it ushers in needless torment, pain, grief, and other negatives that diminish the possibility of such a life—until you understand and believe the promises of God, which He gave us in His Word.

The death of a child—or a loved one at any age—is a traumatic event to overcome. The only way I know to overcome is with God's help. The good news for a born-again believer in Jesus Christ, or for a child who has not reached the age of accountability, is that life does not end with physical death.

"The age of accountability" means that the person has been taught and understands the promises of God in His Word, or at least enough of the Word to be born again. Obviously, a baby or a small child has not had that opportunity, and therefore has not reached what we term "the age of accountability."

At the physical death of a born-again believer, or the physical death of one who has not reached the age of accountability, he or she simply moves to a new location. The moment eyes close and breath ceases in physical death, eyes open and the very next breath comes in the presence of Jesus. That was very comforting news to me!

Jesus confirms this in John 11:25-26 NLT:

> **Jesus told her** [Martha, regarding the death of her brother Lazarus], **"I am the resurrection and the life. Anyone who believes in me will live, even after dying. Everyone who lives in me and believes in me will never ever die...."**

God had nothing to do with Jerry's untimely death. I must admit, though, that at this point in my life, I had the same questions most people have: "Why, Lord? Why my son who whipped every mountain of challenge in the natural?"

I did not share the visitation with anyone until years later. Although I was sedated, I knew everything that was going on and sleep was far from me. [And I might add, never again did I hear Jerry's voice. You can get into some "weird" stuff when you begin to hear voices on a continual basis. I knew this was an infusion of hope, love, and life, God-sent, just for me—not only for the moment, but for the difficult adjustment that was ahead.]

CHAPTER 3

Facing the Reality of the Moment

W HEN YOU ARE IN grief, you need comfort—not people's thoughtless, flippant comments and opinions. You need loved ones and trusted comrades to just "be there"—even if no words are spoken.

At Jerry's wake and funeral, I heard the usual "carnal" words which were supposed to bring comfort:

- "God needed another angel."
- "It was Jerry's time."
- "Jerry has gone through enough suffering."
- "Because you are raising the children of your husband and his previous wife (who passed to heaven months earlier as a result of cancer), it is only fair that she have one of your children!" (Very cruel, cutting words, although the intent of the woman who said this was not vicious, just thoughtless. This type of reasoning cannot be backed up with God's Word.)
- And more....

I was teaching in a community college at the time, and one of the nursing instructors said to me as we stood beside Jerry's casket, "It gets worse." Her words stung. I mean really stung! How could things get worse than this? Then I found out she was speaking from experience. One of her sons, at age fifteen, had died in a farm accident when a pitchfork had pierced his brain.

The only true comfort I received came months after Jerry's death. It was a word to me directly from the Holy Spirit. He said, *When you are together again, it will be as if you were never parted.* To this day, those words comfort me, and I pray they will comfort you as well.

Sometimes I think if we don't know what to say at the death of a loved one or a friend, regardless of the circumstances, or at the birth of a child with special needs, the Apostle Paul's words from Romans 12:15 are appropriate: **"Rejoice with those who rejoice, and weep with those who weep."** To me this means to zip the lip, be a good listener, and let God's compassion flow through you; and allow the Holy Spirit, the Genuine Comforter, to do His work.

CHAPTER 4

Character Development—A Family Affair!

ET'S TAKE A BRIEF look back at Jerry's earlier years. The birth of your first baby usually is an exciting, happy event. Such was the case with Jerry's birth until the doctor said immediately after his birth, "You have a big baby boy [8 lbs., 12 oz.], but he has a cleft lip." That clouded the situation with numerous questions.

When Jerry's condition was diagnosed at the University Hospital in Iowa City, Iowa, he had both a cleft lip and a cleft palate. His surgeries began at three months, then six months, and on and on...

After three turbulent years of marriage, when Jerry was nearly two and I was two months pregnant with his sister, Janet, because of physical abuse from his father, I became a "single mom." Without being asked, at age two Jerry acted like a "little man" and began opening doors for me.

In the absence of his father, one person in particular stepped to the plate to fill the male role in Jerry's life, and that was his Uncle

Mel. Doing farm chores with Mel, even cleaning the pigpens with Mel [scooping manure!!], and going places with him did a great deal to build Jerry's self-esteem. He loved being with Mel. Mel also contributed to Janet's life in many ways. Even to this day, when you are around Mel, you know you are loved and accepted, and you know you are going to have fun and enjoy some humor.

My parents contributed to the lives of both Jerry and Janet (also called "Jan" throughout), taking care of Jan during the times I took Jerry to the hospital. My younger sister Cheryl, who was still in school and living at home, helped with Jan's care too. I will always be grateful for their help. Other family members contributed to their well-being too, but my parents, Mel, and Cheryl were the closest in proximity to have continual input into their lives.

When Jerry was six and Jan three, we moved across the state of Iowa, no longer near family, so I could pursue a college education. Really, this provided an opportunity for both my children and me to pursue a quality education—with Jerry and Jan attending the campus school affiliated with the University of Northern Iowa where I attended classes. The campus school offered educational opportunities that most other schools did not offer at that time.

So what caused me to make a decision to move across the state to enroll in college with no savings, no car, no family nearby, and two precious children?

At this time, I was working part time as a school secretary in the school where I had graduated from high school. One teacher said to me as she walked into the office each morning, "Get out of here and go make something of yourself!" I heard what she had to say, but I didn't know how to make a move with so many obstacles that were seemingly blocking me as a single parent from doing so.

The day came, however, some months later when this teacher walked into the office one morning. Before she could say her usual words of greeting, I held up an envelope addressed to the State College of Iowa [later renamed the University of Northern Iowa], and I said, "Edith, here's my housing deposit for the State College of Iowa." I thought she would fall through the floor! Obviously, she approved, but she was shocked!

That was really the beginning of believing God to move me and my children into a new life, and looking back, I know His hand was on what transpired because it was not possible in the natural. But it was the continual encouragement [and bugging!] of this teacher who stirred me to action for which I will always be grateful.

Settled in our new location, the foundation was being laid for a new life, and during this time Jerry and Jan's lives began to blossom in new ways. [I worked part time and went from no college credits to a Master's degree in four years, so this was our home for these four busy years.]

Jerry developed a friendship with a boy in his class who began life with a cleft lip. In fact, both Jerry and his friend Ross had some of the same doctors and medical professionals at the University of Iowa Hospital.

It was while in this college setting that Jerry had surgery on his palate and at the same time surgery to normalize the outward appearance of his nose. He truly anticipated this surgery with great delight and told his friends, "I'm going to get a new nose!" This surgery contributed much to build Jerry's self-esteem.

After these surgeries, Jerry was on a liquid diet for six weeks. He consumed lots of milk shakes with a raw egg added for protein—until the day he saw me add the egg. Then it was, "Yuck! Regular shakes only, if you please!"

During this same healing time, we took off one afternoon to go fishing—a fun activity for Jerry. [You could put my fishing expertise in a thimble, but I wanted to contribute to my son's fun during his recovery time.] He caught a good-sized fish, and because he was still on a liquid diet, the fish was cleaned and frozen for later eating.

Since money wasn't exactly fluent during "our" college days, we learned to be creative. I remember one Saturday when Jerry and some of his friends wanted to catch butterflies. Jerry didn't have a wire-mesh hoop to catch them, so we made one with a clothes hanger and a yellow pillowcase. It certainly didn't hinder the fun and it worked.

I did not have a car for the first months we were in college, so on Saturdays I would put the laundry basket filled with dirty clothes and Jerry and Jan in our wheels—a wagon—and I would pull the wagon and its precious cargo to the Campus Hill to do laundry. That was a trek of about a mile one way. I had forgotten, but Jan reminded me that the big treat on laundry day was an ice cold Fresca.

When you are grateful, it doesn't take a lot in material things to make you happy! Both Jan and Jerry had thankful hearts.

Jerry and Jan enjoyed the times when we had a "college break," whether for a few days or a week. Once we had a car [which my brother Lowell helped to make possible], we would drive the two hundred miles to my parents' farm home for a change of pace. They always had fun with family and cousins and my mom, being the good cook that she was, always had plenty to eat and lots of treats to enjoy.

Jerry was an excellent student. It's like he had a switch inside of him that he flipped on for each project he did with the attitude, "Give it your best shot!" I still have several of his Social Studies projects of various states and nations, each wonderfully prepared and marked with a grade of "Excellent."

Today, I still have some candy dishes that both Jerry and Janet made in art class at the campus school, plus a turtle that Jerry made, all fired in the school kiln, with their little fingerprints sealed into them.

Church was always a vital part of our lives. During Jerry's hospitalizations we attended nondenominational church services on Sundays that were held in the hospital for whoever wanted to attend—patients as well as family members and/or friends. Usually, as part of these services, communion was explained and served. Jerry was always an eager participant, acknowledging that God Almighty was his God and Jesus was his Lord and Savior.

We also attended our local church regularly, which played a huge role in building Jerry's character and confidence and in understanding God's love for him.

During "our" college years, Jerry was privileged to be a guest at one of the church's father-son banquets, with his host being a leading businessman in the city who was also a key leader in the church we attended.

In Hebrews 13:5 NLT God promises, **"I will never fail you. I will never abandon you."** The *Amplified Bible, Classic Edition* of this verse says, **"For He [God] Himself has said, I will not in any way fail you nor give you up nor leave you without support. [I will] not, [I will] not, [I will] not in any degree leave you helpless nor forsake nor let [you] down (relax My hold on you)! [Assuredly not!]"**

God keeps His promises. He provided godly male models for Jerry to emulate on several occasions.

CHAPTER 5

Packing
Life with Love

N SPITE OF JERRY'S numerous hospitalizations and surgeries, he did a whole lot of living in twelve short years. He was writing his own newspaper when he was in fourth grade and selling it for one or two cents a copy.

The newspaper always contained jokes as well as poems, tongue twisters, and brief articles of current news events which he summarized. Here is a sample of the jokes from one of his newspapers:

- *What kind of shoes are made out of banana skins?* (Slippers.)
- *What color would you paint the sun and the wind?* (The sun rose and the wind blue.)
- *To what man does everyone always take off their hat?* (The barber.)
- *What did one tonsil say to the other tonsil?* (Get dressed! The doctor is taking us out tonight.)
- *What is the worst weather for rats and mice?* (When it rains cats and dogs.)

I don't know the source of his jokes, but his newspaper was always interesting, well organized, and creative.

Both Jerry and Jan made their own greeting cards for all occasions. Often, the card contained a paper window which you could open to a special message, such as, "I love you." Again, with both Jerry and Jan, their cards were very creative and "from the heart." As their mom, my perspective is that they could have given card companies some tough competition!

At times, when it was someone's birthday, Jerry would pick a recipe [he never used a box mix], purchase the items that weren't in the cupboard with his own money, and turn into a mighty fine chef. Nothing ever seemed too challenging for him.

I was the recipient of some of his baking projects. For one of my birthdays, Jerry asked that I go upstairs and stay there while he did something special. [It was a Sunday afternoon, and I had student papers to correct, so I spent the afternoon grading them "upstairs," away from the kitchen area.]

Jerry took Jan with him to the store on his bike, purchased items I did not have to make a chiffon cake [a difficult recipe I'm not sure I would have tried], made the cake, frosted it, and then I was escorted to the kitchen to enjoy the finished product. And it was absolutely first class!

You could say that Jerry's taste buds were keen early on! It was after his first surgery at three months that he and I were with my parents on a blistering hot summer day. We stopped for ice cream cones. Obviously, Jerry was a little young for ice cream, but I let him lick it. His orientation to ice cream was a big hit! When there were no more "licks," he cried. From that day forth, ice cream was a favorite!

When I was gone for two-day conferences or to state competitive events with my college students, usually my mother stayed with Jerry and Jan. I always came home to a surprise. On one occasion it was a gingerbread cookie, plate-size, baked, frosted, and decorated, which Jerry and Jan had made.

Jerry was a young entrepreneur as well! At age ten, he walked his paper route early in the mornings. On rare occasions, when it was raining or snowing, I would drive him on his route. Because of this, my Christmas present that year was a beautiful white rug with a note attached:

> *"This rug is to put*
> *in front of your bed*
> *so if you have to get up at 5:30*
> *your feet will be warm.*
> *——Jerry and Janet"*

How's that for love and thoughtfulness?

I remember an evening when Jerry and some of the other paper carriers met with their supervisor to go door-to-door, soliciting new subscriptions to the paper. The carrier who got the most subscriptions would receive a new hoodie. Jerry came home grinning from ear to ear with the prize in hand for his efforts—a new navy blue hoodie!

Jerry was always thoughtful, considerate, and loving.

Whatever he did, he put his heart and soul into it. He contributed enormously to the reality of celebrating life. It didn't just come from me to my children. Jerry was a major contributor to the joys we experienced and so was Jan.

If something didn't seem right to him, Jerry would challenge me, although he never disrespected me. For example, it was a ten-minute drive from my work to our house and Jerry and Jan's school was a block and a half from our house; so most days we would meet at home and have lunch together.

On one occasion, our fruit for lunch was canned plums. They were not Jerry's favorite, so he said, as he made faces while eating them, "What did your mother feed you that made you like everything so much?" He was working for an alibi so he wouldn't have to eat the plums! I wouldn't have made him eat them if they were that distasteful to him, but he ate them while waiting for my response to his question!

When together for family events, Jerry, Jan, and their cousins would create and color a movie on shelf paper or unused wallpaper and roll it through a cardboard screen they made so everyone in attendance could enjoy "the movie." At these times, there was so much laughter and joy that I'm sure the roof of the house, if not intact, could have danced to our hilarity!

Prior to his death, Jerry had just completed his confirmation class at church. He had built solid friendships with a few of his classmates, and he was developing into a fine young man.

With the hospital his second home for the first years of his life, it had a strong influence on what he talked about as his career choice for when he was older. He always said that he wanted to become a doctor *so he could help people.* [Although he was denied a medical career because of his premature death, I sent the savings from his paper route to his surgeon earmarked "for medical research," as I knew he was involved in a research project at the time. I'm sure Jerry would have approved, as he had high respect for all of the medical professionals who were involved in his surgeries and treatments.]

In our trips to the hospital, we always saw suffering that was worse than the challenges Jerry was walking through. Jerry's view of what he was going through was an attitude of "I'll whip this, and then it will be behind me!" Jerry's beautiful, positive, and confident attitude always contributed to his ability to overcome every challenge.

CHAPTER 6

Overcoming Grief

GOD'S LOVE, DEMONSTRATED THROUGH you and me in our words and actions [primarily in our actions with few words spoken], will help to comfort and free others of grief, pain, torment, guilt, and the negatives they are going through after the death of their loved one.

Months after Jerry's death, I stopped at the grocery store after work to pick up a few items. I had my cart partially filled when I saw his band instructor across the aisles.

Jerry was privileged in that coming into this school district from a campus school, he was one year ahead of the other students in his class in band. As a result, he was the only sixth grader in the city to be selected to be in the All-City Elementary Band. This was a very distinct honor for him.

On the Sunday afternoon of the All-City Band Concert, Jerry played the drums in style—with an attitude! Like other things he did, he put himself totally into it. I'll never forget the joy that radiated from his face that day. He performed in an excellent manner and he knew it.

We celebrated after the concert by enjoying one of his favorites—ice cream!

Back to the grocery store and seeing his band instructor...

When I saw his band instructor, I tried to hold back the tears, but I couldn't. I felt no reprimand from God for letting the tears flow, because at this point in my life, I did not understand the promises in the Word of God regarding life after death. I have found that we can be much too callous with our words and actions when we've never walked through such an experience.

Grief literally enshrouded me during the months following Jerry's death, again because I did not know God's Word regarding life after death for the born-again believer and for little ones who have not reached the age of accountability. I continued to fill the roles of teacher, wife, and mother, but the heaviness of grief accompanied me in everything I did. I still deeply missed my champion of a son, Jerry Paul.

Although I had been in church all my life, I had never been taught the eternal hope from God's Word regarding physical death for believers in Jesus Christ—that you literally go from life to life. But now, God had my ear like never before!

I'm sure I had heard Second Corinthians 5:8 before, but suddenly it came alive to me in a completely new way: **"To be absent from the body and to be present with the Lord."** The *New Living Translation* words it this way: **"Yes, we are fully confident, and we would rather be away from these earthly bodies, for then we will be at home with the Lord."** This is a promise for every born-again believer and for those who have not yet reached the age of accountability.

I learned that at physical death, or cessation of breath, the spirit and soul of a born-again person go immediately into the presence of the Lord. The soul is made up of the mind, will, and emotions. The spirit of the born-again believer [or the inner man] is where the Holy Spirit abides. At physical death, the outer man [a person's body] is the part that is buried in the grave until the rapture of the Church.

In First Thessalonians 4:13-18 NLT, Paul gives us eternal hope regarding physical death:

> And now, dear brothers and sisters, we want you to know what will happen to the believers who have died so you will not grieve like people who have no hope. For since we believe that Jesus died and was raised to life again, we also believe that when Jesus returns, God will bring back with him the believers who have died.
>
> We tell you this directly from the Lord: We who are still living when the Lord returns will not meet him ahead of those who have died. For the Lord himself will come down from heaven with a commanding shout, with the voice of the archangel, and with the trumpet call of God. First, the believers who have died will rise from their graves. Then, together with them, we who are still alive and remain on the earth will be caught up in the clouds to meet the Lord in the air. Then we will be with the Lord forever. So encourage each other with these words.

We are not without hope, for Numbers 23:19 tells us, **"God is not a man, that He should lie, nor a son of man, that He should** repent. Has He said, and will He not do? Or has He spoken, and will He not make it good?"

My son and your loved one [born again or not having reached the age of accountability yet] who have tasted physical death, are in the presence of the Lord.

Thank God for His goodness and for the Holy Spirit's comfort. Because of Jesus, we are not without hope. When I believed God and His Word, trusted Him, and thanked Him for His eternal love plan, grief left me, although it was a process. I learned that you can still enjoy the precious memories of your loved one who has arrived in heaven ahead of you. But your focus should be on Jesus first and foremost, then on celebrating life with your loved ones and others who need your love and your input into their lives now.

It was during this time that a friend told me about the baptism with the Holy Spirit. I wanted all of Jesus I could get, so once I understood what it meant, I received the empowerment from this experience [see Acts 1:8 and Acts, chapter 2]. This baptism strengthened me daily to deal with life's issues that I was facing from God's perspective—and still strengthens me daily.

Life improved when I looked to Jesus and cast my hurts, pains, cares, grief, guilt, shame, condemnation, and other negatives upon Him as First Peter 5:7 AMP says:

> Casting the whole of your care [all your anxieties, all your worries, all your concerns, once and for all] on Him, for He cares for you affectionately and cares about you watchfully.

Jesus will heal your heart as you release your anxieties, worries, and concerns to Him; and He will bring "new life" to you in the way that is most meaningful to you.

One child can never replace another, but I experienced new life when I gave birth to a baby girl three years after Jerry's death. And what that new baby didn't know is that she was the fulfillment of a desire of my heart!

During our "college days," occasionally Jerry, Janet, and I would take a short evening drive for a change of pace. On about a quarter's worth of gas, we couldn't go too far! I would tell them that one of my heart's desires was to marry and have one more child.

Psalm 37:4 AMPC says: **"Delight yourself also in the Lord, and He will give you the desires and secret petitions of your heart."** He has proven Himself faithful to me again and again!

CHAPTER 7

Celebrating My Children

G OD HAS A WAY of turning sorrow into joy and ushering in new life. Janet, the first of my two daughters, was born when Jerry was about two-and-a-half years old, and as I mentioned previously, Brenda was born three years after Jerry's death.

While carrying Jan in my womb, I consistently prayed that she would be a healthy baby because of the medical challenges I faced with my son. When she made her appearance at 11:03 a.m. on December 2, 1959, she was a healthy, beautiful baby.

Jan, like Jerry, excelled as a student. Today, Jan is a wife, a mother, a grandma, and a day care director. Her husband Jay is in sales and marketing of boat docks and services. Jan and her husband are the parents of two daughters, Jessica and Jennifer.

Jessica, their oldest, taught kindergarten for six years and then completed her doctorate degree in Early Child Education. While finishing her doctorate, she gave birth to their first child, a baby boy, Liam Jack. Today Jessica is still employed in Early Child

Education, and she gave birth to a baby girl, Emma Kate, in April of 2018. Her husband Colt is a youth pastor.

Jenny, my second granddaughter, is a registered nurse, and her husband Brad is an investment advisor. At the time of this writing, Jenny has given birth to their first child, a boy, Reese Anderson Rollins.

My stepson, Brad, is a very successful business executive. He and his wife Lori have two grown children, Michael and Mindy, with families of their own. [Brad's sister, Terry, passed away in 2016.]

Brenda brought new life to me when she made her appearance. The truth is, she literally brought new life to our entire neighborhood! When we came home from the hospital, the kids in our neighborhood were so excited at the thought of seeing the new baby that they lined up at our front door. How do you turn away several "curious, bubbly kids" who want to be part of this happy event? We let them come through the front door, parade style to see the baby, and then go out through the garage to keep the event orderly.

Brenda, inquisitive and loving, at three and four years of age, enjoyed helping in the kitchen—with her fingers in the cookie dough, etc. Today she is an outstanding cook. Believe me, her culinary arts go beyond the cookie dough days!

Brenda, like Jerry and Jan, excelled in her studies. She has an exceptionally strong anointing in dealing with babies and children. Today, she is using that gifting in her career as a speech language pathologist on four levels—elementary, middle school, high school, and college.

Brenda never misses an opportunity to bring laughter to any setting. Recently, as I was cleaning out a drawer of notes and cards received in the past, I came across a Mother's Day card from her which says:

> *In honor of Mother's Day, I ran the dishwasher!*
> *And since there was some room on the top shelf,*
> *I did some socks and underwear, too!*
> *I love you, Brenda*

Although she would never do that in the natural, how can you have a sad heart with that kind of input for hilarity?

On another occasion, Brenda told me about a magazine article she had read, which gives justification health-wise for NOT making your bed each day! The article said that an unmade bed may help you breathe easier. A study suggested that microscopic dust mites—implicated in some respiratory problems—are less likely to survive in an unmade bed.

Brenda's conclusion: *"If we don't make our bed, we are really taking better care of ourselves! We are contributing to our own health! So just throw your covers back and head out the door!!!"*

There are many things we can do to get out of the "mullygrubs" of sorrow and grief, although it takes an effort. One is to keep the laughter going!

Laughter is a great healing agent as Proverbs 17:22 AMPC says: **"A happy heart is good medicine and a cheerful mind works healing, but a broken spirit dries up the bones."**

The baggage from a grief-filled heart and mind does not contribute to the wellness of the body and soul [mind, will, and emotions].

It is each person's choice to be peaceful, happy, and joyful. Others will benefit from this type of attitude, but you will be the greatest beneficiary of such an attitude.

One more suggestion in celebrating my children, or any other person for that matter. I had to learn to listen to the heart of my children as well as to their words.

CHAPTER 8

Our Loved Ones in Heaven See Our "Spiritual Progress"

NOTHER HUGE SPARK OF hope and comfort ignited into full flames within me years after Jerry's death while I was in attendance at a Winter Bible Seminar at Kenneth Hagin Ministries. The speaker suddenly took a "side trip" from his main topic. He shared how our loved ones in heaven can see our spiritual progress—not our natural progress—but what is going on with us spiritually. This agrees with the scripture from Hebrews 12:1-2 NLT:

> **Therefore, since we are surrounded by such a huge crowd of witnesses [the saints in heaven] to the life of faith, let us strip off every weight that slows us down, especially the sin that so easily trips us up. And let us run with endurance the race God has set before us. We do this by keeping our eyes on Jesus, the champion who initiates and perfects our faith. . . .**

By this time in my walk with the Lord, I realized that grief, and unforgiveness as well, are weights that would slow me down, hold me back, and even shipwreck me in an attempt to keep me from running and completing the spiritual race God had set before me.

Another area that needed my attention was the love walk—with all people of all ages, races, and cultures. I found that the love walk will solve a lot of issues, and would set me free to blossom in my own life. The best description of this kind of love—*agape*, the God-kind of love—that I have found is in First Corinthians 13:4-8. Let's look at it from *The Amplified Bible, Classic Edition:*

> Love endures long and is patient and kind; love never is envious nor boils over with jealousy, is not boastful or vainglorious, does not display itself haughtily.
>
> It is not conceited (arrogant and inflated with pride); it is not rude (unmannerly) and does not act unbecomingly. Love (God's love in us) does not insist on its own rights or its own way, for it is not self-seeking; it is not touchy or fretful or resentful; it takes no account of the evil done to it [it pays no attention to a suffered wrong].
>
> It does not rejoice at injustice and unrighteousness, but rejoices when right and truth prevail.
>
> Love bears up under anything and everything that comes, is ever ready to believe the best of every person, its hopes are fadeless under all circumstances, and it endures everything [without weakening].
>
> Love never fails [never fades out or becomes obsolete or comes to an end]....

I found that it's a choice to be free of all weights—grief, bitterness, ill will, resentment, unforgiveness, and/or any other negatives—by letting the God-kind of love dominate me.

I want to cause my loved ones who have filled the grandstands of heaven to rejoice with great exuberance—not just when I arrive in heaven—but today because of earthly accomplishments for God and His Kingdom. There's no person or situation that can hold you or me back unless we allow it by getting out of the love walk.

I have decided to go for the gold, meaning to go for God's best in all that I say and do by giving Him my all. I am determined to keep my loved ones in heaven rejoicing over my spiritual progress, and I am determined to celebrate life every day with my loved ones and others while here in the earth.

CHAPTER 9

Forgive!
Forgive! Forgive!

U NLESS SOMEONE HAS WALKED through the death of a loved
one or suffered a painful separation from a loved one,
they cannot fully understand the pain that you or I have
gone through or that we are presently going through, but Jesus
fully understands. And regardless of the situation that caused our
loved one's death, or the separation, we must forgive ourselves as
well as others for mistakes or misjudgments made or for situations
that were out of our control.

If we are in a situation that we do not understand or that does
not make sense as to why our loved one passed on to heaven, we
can trust God's Word that says, **"The secret things belong to the
Lord our God..."** (Deuteronomy 29:29). I made a decision to not
camp on the "whys," but to trust God, knowing that He would
reveal to me the things I needed to know.

I understood that I couldn't fully celebrate the lives of my
spouse or other children, siblings, parents, relatives, coworkers,
or anyone else unless my heart was free of unforgiveness. I can

guarantee you, life will offer plenty of opportunities to experience hurt, disappointment, and offense, but it is a choice to live above it by forgiving and releasing the perpetrator(s). It was my choice to live as a victim or as a victor. It was my choice to forgive and release others. It was my choice to attempt to be better rather than bitter as a result of what I had experienced.

In numerous situations I have faced in life, I have found myself asking the Lord, "When is he [or she] going to repent and apologize for the gross injustice that was done to me?" In one situation, when the sting of the pain wasn't quite as potent, the Holy Spirit spoke to me, and said:

> *True forgiveness is to forgive and release the person [or offender] and the incident [the offense] whether the person ever apologizes to you or not.*

That shocked me. God's Word, all of it, is a message from the heart of God so we can grow in His wisdom and become more like Him as we read it, meditate on it, and obey it. His Word says, **"Avenge not yourselves... Vengeance is Mine; I will repay, saith the Lord"** (Romans 12:19 KJV). Then I read verses 17-21 from the *New Living Translation:*

> **Never pay back evil with more evil. Do things in such a way that everyone can see you are honorable. Do all that you can to live in peace with everyone.**
>
> **Dear friends, never take revenge. Leave that to the righteous anger of God. For the Scriptures say, "I will take revenge; I will pay them back," says the Lord.**

Instead, "If your enemies are hungry, feed them. If they are thirsty, give them something to drink. In doing this, you will heap burning coals of shame on their heads."

Don't let evil conquer you, but <u>conquer evil by doing good.</u>

In other words, regardless of the reason for Jerry's premature death, I needed to take inventory of my own life. I needed to shut any doors that were open to the enemy because of unforgiveness, resentment, and/or bitterness in my own heart.

As I continued to fill myself daily with portions of God's Word, it helped to build "substance" within me and strengthened me to react to situations as Jesus would (as I allowed my spirit to dominate my flesh) with the God-kind of grace, mercy, wisdom, and love.

To let God be the vengeance giver in my life meant to set those responsible for the harm done to me completely free, with not one thought of malice in my heart to get back at them. <u>To me, it meant blessing them, which would release God to be God in my behalf as well as in their behalf.</u>

In Mark 11:25-26, Jesus tells us the importance of forgiveness:

"**And whenever you stand praying, if you have anything against anyone, forgive him, that your Father in heaven may also forgive you your trespasses.**

"**But if you do not forgive, neither will your Father in heaven forgive your trespasses.**"

In other words, the quicker I forgave and released anyone who had hurt me, even if it seemed like it was blatant and purposeful, the quicker I would be liberated to live a life of purpose and peace. I knew that God wanted me to be blessed and prospered in every area of my life, but I wouldn't realize the fullness of it until my own heart was free of unforgiveness. *Forgiving and releasing others, whether I thought they deserved it or not, were keys to my own freedom and wholeness!*

The only effective way I know to overcome grief, whatever the cause of it, is through an intimate relationship with Jesus Christ. When accepting Jesus Christ as our personal Savior and Lord, First John 4:4 says, "**He** [Jesus Christ] **who is in you is greater than he** [the devil] **who is in the world.**" As a born-again believer, not only was Jesus in me in the Person of the Holy Spirit, but I finally understood that He loved me, He was for me, and He would never forsake me.

If I truly love Jesus and want to be like Him, my heart motive toward any offender should be, "Lord, how can I help this person be all You want him or her to be and blossom in their life here on earth?" If that is my heart motive, then I will be freed up to blossom in my own life.

By "blossoming," I mean to be able to accomplish extraordinary exploits in life that would affect multitudes of people for great good as well as complete my own God-ordained destiny in excellence.

Most of us have heard the old but true saying, "Hang out with those you want to become like!" In my opinion, the coolest Person you can hang out with is Jesus!

One of Jerry's Childhood Prayers

When Jerry and Jan were together with cousins, often they played school. One of Jerry's activities during this time was to write prayers, expressing what was in his heart to God. Following is one of those prayers, written when he was about eight years old.

Although written from a child's point of view, it contains sincere requests and thanksgiving, appropriate for any of us at any age!

Dear God

Help me to forgive, others
help me to do whats right
thank you for sisters and Brothers
thank you for day and night
help me to be clean
and help me to be nice
Thank you for food like lean
bananas and other like rice Amen

Prayer of Release and Forgiveness

Here is a sample prayer that I have used as a guide in forgiving and releasing offenders and letting go of offenses.

Father God, I acknowledge that You had nothing to do with the premature death of my loved one. You are the Author of abundant life, and it is the devil who steals, kills, and destroys. Forgive me for thinking You were teaching me something through this tragedy or maturing me through it. I now realize *that You teach, train, and discipline Your children through Your Word and Your Holy Spirit. You <u>never</u> use Satan's works to teach, train, and discipline Your children.*

Although there are some things I do not understand about the premature death of my loved one, I release the entire situation to You, Jesus—my broken heart and the grief, sorrow, and pain—and I receive Your peace, healing, and wholeness.

Thank You that my loved one is with You, Lord, and that we will be together again—and once reunited, there will be no remembrance of the time of separation from each other.

I recommit myself completely to You, Lord, so You are free to orchestrate my life and realign it perfectly with Your agenda. I love You, Lord, and through the power You have invested in me, I will run to finish the course You have set for me— imitating You, the Champion of all champions, my Lord and Savior Jesus Christ. Amen.

CHAPTER 10

A Personal Exam

K NOWING WHAT I KNOW today, I now realize that to grieve for a long time over anyone's death is selfishness. Why? Your focus is primarily on you. It's not on God and it's not on your loved ones who need you. Plus, grief will not contribute to your well-being physically, mentally, emotionally, or spiritually. To carry grief is really an act of unbelief once you understand that Jesus already paid the price for your griefs and sorrows. However, just as physical healing often is a process, getting beyond grief often is a process as well.

Many Christians have never been taught that during His crucifixion on the cross at Calvary, besides paying the penalty in full for our sins, Jesus paid for our griefs and sorrows, sickness and disease, poverty and lack, and spiritual death.

Each person needs time to work through the grief they are experiencing, which will be different for each person. The primary key is that we should not grieve as the world grieves, because we are not without hope. In Jesus Christ, we do have hope.

I appreciate the clear understanding of First Thessalonians 4:13-18 in the *Amplified Bible, Classic Edition,* and I believe you will too. [I quoted it earlier from the *New Living Translation.*]

> Now also we would not have you ignorant, brethren, about those who fall asleep [in death], that you may not grieve [for them] as the rest do who have no hope [beyond the grave].
>
> For since we believe that Jesus died and rose again, even so God will also bring with Him through Jesus those who have fallen asleep [in death].
>
> For this we declare to you by the Lord's [own] word, that we who are alive and remain until the coming of the Lord shall in no way precede [into His presence] or have any advantage at all over those who have previously fallen asleep [in Him in death].
>
> For the Lord Himself will descend from heaven with a loud cry of summons, with the shout of an archangel, and with the blast of the trumpet of God. And those who have departed this life in Christ will rise first.
>
> Then we, the living ones who remain [on the earth], shall simultaneously be caught up along with [the resurrected dead] in the clouds to meet the Lord in the air; and so always (through the eternity of the eternities) we shall be with the Lord!
>
> Therefore comfort and encourage one another with these words.

God did not create anyone to carry pain, grief, or sorrow. The price Jesus paid on Calvary's cross includes payment in full for pain—physical, mental, and emotional—and this includes grief and sorrow.

> Surely He [Jesus] has borne our griefs (sicknesses, weaknesses, and distresses) and carried our sorrows and pains [of punishment], yet we [ignorantly] considered Him stricken, smitten, and afflicted by God [as if with leprosy].
> But He was wounded for our transgressions, He was bruised for our guilt and iniquities; the chastisement [needful to obtain] peace and well-being for us was upon Him, and with the stripes [that wounded] Him we are healed and made whole.
> —Isaiah 53:4-5 AMPC

The quicker we can come to terms with what we cannot change in the natural, the quicker we will be able to get back on course and complete the destiny to which God has called us.

I believe it is God's plan that we live, love, and laugh again on a higher level, certainly not because of the tragedy, trauma, and heartache we have experienced, but because of our renewed love relationship with Jesus Christ.

CHAPTER 11

So How Do We "Get Out of Ourselves"?

O NE OF THE REASONS many people have a challenge in adjusting to death, even the death of a person who has lived out the fullness of their days, is the fear of death—not realizing that there is hope beyond the grave for believers in Jesus Christ [as well as for babies and children who have not reached the age of accountability].

Hosea 4:6 says, **"My people are destroyed for lack of knowl-edge...."** This verse also indicates that destruction can come because of "rejection" of the knowledge of God's Word.

At the time of my son's death, I did not understand God's prom-ises regarding what happens to a born-again believer or a baby, child, or person who has not reached the age of accountability at the moment of death. Yet I had been in church since I was a small child. Therefore, the torment and harassment of the enemy were very strong. It was only when I began to understand and believe the promises of God regarding physical death and the spiritual principles of His Word that the healing process began in me. I also had to make a decision that my flesh would no longer rule me. I would allow the Spirit of God to rule me.

Initially, you might have thought that Jerry's grave site was a shrine to me, for I visited his grave nearly every morning before I went to work. What motivated me to do this was the enemy's torment. I had no peace in my heart, and it was my "connection," if you could call it that, in those first few weeks and months for handling the shock of Jerry's sudden death.

As I began to understand the truths of God's Word, I realized that Jerry's body was in the grave, but his spirit and soul were with Jesus in heaven. [Your spirit and soul depart to be with Jesus at the very moment of physical death.]

A truth from God's Word that comforted me is from Hebrews 13:5: **"I will never leave you nor forsake you."**

God's love for you and me is unchanging. One of the first scriptures that became revelation to me of God's love for me was Exodus 19:5: **"If you will indeed obey My voice and keep My covenant, then you shall be a <u>special treasure</u> to Me above all people...."**

God's Word is life-filled and life-giving, so I began to confess the promises of His Word over myself, my spouse, my children, and others. For example, using this scripture as a foundation, I believed and confessed: *Because I love the Lord and obey His Word, which is His will, I am a special treasure to Him. Because my spouse and my children love and obey the Lord, each is a special treasure unto the Lord as well.*

God loves you and me, and He values us beyond what we can think or even imagine. We can't love others as we should without knowing God's excessive and unconditional love for us, His children. And we can't expect to draw the only type of love that will fill the emptiness in our heart and heal the pain and brokenness we have experienced from another human being.

Although we need loved ones to affirm us, Jesus alone is the Healer of the broken heart. In Luke 4:18 Jesus said, "**He** [God the Father] **has sent Me to heal the brokenhearted. . . .**"

What we do for others will come back to us in like kind and in like measure. The God-kind of love—*agape*—should be our motivation for getting out of ourselves and celebrating others.

A beautiful example of this type of love came just a few days after Jerry's homegoing celebration, when suddenly I noticed one of his closest friends, Paul, and his mother walking up the driveway. With a beautiful cup filled with fresh flowers in his hands and tears splashing down his cheeks, Paul's mother and I couldn't hold back the tears either. Not a lot of words were spoken, because the demonstration of love was loud and clear. Paul, like Jerry, was a kind, caring young man. He reached beyond his own pain to demonstrate the God-kind of love to me and my family. That's an example of getting out of yourself!

My oldest sister, Ann, is no stranger to grief as her husband passed away a few years ago. Today, when someone passes away in her community, she, being a marvelous cook, bakes cookie bars or other treats, or takes a meat and cheese tray to share with the grieving family to contribute to their fellowship time. She is continually reaching out to others with the God-kind of love in this manner. That's another example of "getting out of yourself."

We will not stay in grief as we learn to celebrate others; and as we look for opportunities to be a blessing to someone else, our own pain will dissipate, and we will, more than likely, end up being the most blessed!

CHAPTER 12

Using Our
God-given Authority

G OD HAS GIVEN EVERY born-again believer authority. It's
time that we rise up and use it as never before against
the enemy whose purpose is to steal, kill, and destroy.
(See John 10:10.)

In Luke 10:19 Jesus said, **"Behold, I give you the authority to
trample on serpents and scorpions, and <u>over all the power of the
enemy</u>, and nothing shall by any means hurt you."** [As a point of
clarification, "serpents and scorpions" in this verse refer to any act
of the enemy, the devil.]

There are two forces at work in the earth: the devil and the Lord.
As you and I bind the enemy [the devil] over our own life, our
loved ones, and the lives of those for whom we are praying, the
antics and the fury of the enemy can be stopped. Totally stopped!

Today, I better understand the authority that God has given me
as a born-again believer, and I use that authority in my prayer life
before my feet hit the floor each morning.

For example, I daily plead the blood of Jesus Christ over each
of my family members, siblings and their families, and others as
the Holy Spirit leads.

This is essentially what I pray:

Father, I plead the blood of Jesus Christ over _____'s body, soul [this includes the mind, will, and emotions], and spirit; and over his/her property, finances, relationships, and reputation. Thank You, Jesus, for being Lord and Savior of each of our lives. Thank You for the power in Your shed blood and for the privilege of using Your name, Your blood, and Your Word in prayer. I exalt You above all, Jesus, and I thank You for Your sacrifice for all mankind, giving every person a choice to receive You as Savior and Lord.

I honor my Heavenly Father daily by praying Matthew 6:9-13:

Our Father in heaven, hallowed be Your name.
Your kingdom come. Your will be done on earth [and in each person for whom I am praying] **as it is in heaven.**
Give us this day our daily bread.
And forgive us our debts, as we forgive our debtors.
And do not lead us into temptation, but deliver us from the evil one.
For Yours is the kingdom and the power and the glory FOREVER. Amen. [Emphasis mine.]

I call Satan's bluff in prayer! More than once in more than one situation, I have decreed, *"Satan, enough is enough! Stop your devious efforts in this person's life now in Jesus' name."*

To call Satan's bluff means to agree with God's Word, believe it, and speak His Word promises instead of rehearsing and repeating negative circumstances. Jesus has already redeemed every born-again believer from the curse of the law (Galatians 3:13), but we have to know it, believe it, and then act upon it. The curse of the law includes sickness and disease, tragedies and calamities, poverty and lack, and spiritual death—anything contrary to God's nature.

I frame loved ones with what God says about them in His Word to avoid a tragedy, a calamity, a health crisis, or any other negative work of the enemy. I do it as a part of my daily prayer lifestyle. To "frame" a person means to speak the life-giving promises of God's Word over them. Here are a few examples:

- Psalm 5:12—*Thank You, Lord, that You surround _____ with Your favor as with a shield.*

- Isaiah 54:14—*Thank You, Lord, that _____ is established in righteousness. He/she is far from oppression and does not fear, for terror will not come near _____ .*

- Isaiah 54:17—*No weapon formed against _____ shall prosper. Every tongue that rises against him/her in judgment, he/she shall condemn.* [Condemn the person's words, not the person!]

- 2 Timothy 1:7—*God has not given _____ a spirit of fear, but a spirit of power, love, and a sound mind in Jesus' name.*

- 1 Corinthians 2:16—*_____ has the mind of Christ.*

- 3 John 2—*_____ prospers and enjoys good health, even as his/her soul prospers.*

- Jeremiah 29:11—*God's thoughts of _____ are of peace and not of evil, to give him/her a future and a hope.*
- Ephesians 6:1-3—*_____ is obedient to his/her parents, and he/she honors them. As a result, things will go well for _____, and he/she will have a long life on the earth.*
- Isaiah 49:16 NLT—*Thank You, Father, that You have written _____'s name on the palms of Your hands.*

The Word of God has a lot to say about framing our children, families, and others with the words we are speaking. Proverbs 18:21 says, **"Death and life are in the power of the tongue, and those who love it will eat its fruit."** Proverbs 6:2 says, **"You are snared by the words of your mouth; you are taken by the words of your mouth."**

Job 22:28 KJV says, **"Thou shalt also decree a thing, and it shall be established unto thee...."**

God created with the words of His mouth. Hebrews 11:3 says, **"By faith we understand that the worlds were framed by the word of God, so that the things which are seen were not made of things which are visible."**

We, too, can create positive or negative situations with the words of our mouth.

Since we are dealing specifically with premature death, decree each day: *Because my children are covered with the blood of Jesus, no harm, tragedy, or calamity will come to them in Jesus' name. Thank You, Father, for directing my children by Your precious Holy Spirit.*

Thank You that You order Your angels to protect them wherever they go. I also thank You, Father, for giving me wisdom, as a parent/guardian, to guide my children in the way You would have them go in Jesus' name.

Psalm 91 Promises

To better understand our authority and to agree with the promises of God to protect our loved ones, here are the promises of Psalm 91 from the *Amplified Bible, Classic Edition*. Personally, I pray this Psalm over my loved ones and myself daily:

> He who dwells in the secret place of the Most High shall remain stable and fixed under the shadow of the Almighty [Whose power no foe can withstand].
>
> I will say of the Lord, He is my Refuge and my Fortress, my God; on Him I lean and rely, and in Him I [confidently] trust!
>
> For [then] He will deliver you from the snare of the fowler and from the deadly pestilence.
>
> [Then] He will cover you with His pinions, and under His wings shall you trust and find refuge; His truth and His faithfulness are a shield and a buckler.
>
> You shall not be afraid of the terror of the night, nor of the arrow (the evil plots and slanders of the wicked) that flies by day,
>
> Nor of the pestilence that stalks in darkness, nor of the destruction and sudden death that surprise and lay waste at noonday.
>
> A thousand may fall at your side, and ten thousand at your right hand, but it shall not come near you.

Only a spectator shall you be [yourself inaccessible in the secret place of the Most High] as you witness the reward of the wicked.

Because you have made the Lord your refuge, and the Most High your dwelling place,

There shall no evil befall you, nor any plague or calamity come near your tent.

For He will give His angels [especial] charge over you to accompany and defend and preserve you in all your ways [of obedience and service].

They shall bear you up on their hands, lest you dash your foot against a stone.

You shall tread upon the lion and adder; the young lion and the serpent shall you trample underfoot.

Because he has set his love upon Me, therefore will I deliver him; I will set him on high, because he knows and understands My name [has a personal knowledge of My mercy, love, and kindness—trusts and relies on Me, knowing I will never forsake him, no, never].

He shall call upon Me, and I will answer him; I will be with him in trouble, I will deliver him and honor him.

With long life will I satisfy him and show him My salvation.

Thank You, Father God, for Your promises of protection, provision, wisdom, grace, love, and mercy to every person who submits to You and obeys You in Jesus' name.

CHAPTER 13

Final Thoughts:
A Life of Courage

"So be strong and courageous! Do not be afraid and do not panic... For the Lord your God will personally go ahead of you. He will neither fail you nor abandon you."
—Deuteronomy 31:6 NLT

HERE IS A REVIEW of Jerry's short life. What a mighty demonstration of courage he gave to our family and to all who knew him!

- At three months, Jerry had his first surgery. This surgery connected one nostril and the lip area associated with it. [The substance of the nostril and lip was there, but it was not connected.]
- Three months later, at six months, the second nostril and lip area were connected surgically.
- Major surgery on the palate.
- Major surgery to reconstruct the outward appearance of his nose at nine years of age.

- Several myringotomies throughout the years—a procedure where an incision is made in the eardrum to create an artificial opening to relieve pressure and allow drainage of fluid from an inflamed middle ear.

- Insertion of tubes in his ears periodically between the ages of six and nine to help normalize his hearing. [Also wore a hearing aid for two years to enhance his hearing.]

- Removal of his tonsils and adenoids [completed in two separate surgeries].

- Removal of top front teeth because of abscessing. Replaced with a partial. Wore braces to help with proper alignment of his other teeth.

- And more....

All of these surgeries and medical procedures were like trials and tests of courage and character. If Jerry could step to the plate for each of these surgeries and procedures without fear, there is nothing we cannot overcome as we look to Jesus, and live and move and have our being in Him—His wisdom, grace, mercy, love, and favor. (See Acts 17:28.)

We had invited the Lord to be a part of our daily lives, and we leaned upon Him for His help, guidance, wisdom, strength, and healing virtue for each surgical and medical procedure. His touch upon Jerry's life gave him extraordinary courage, and his recoveries were always quick and complete.

Jerry was strong when teased by others and called "flat nose." That was like a curse word of the worst kind after all of the surgeries he had been through, but when God is not in control of your flesh [your mouth and your actions], whatever comes to mind usually is expressed regardless of your age.

While reminiscing, my momma's heart wanted to hug my son and tell him one more time, "I love you"! I wasn't ready to say good-bye to my only son, my firstborn, one who was an overcomer in natural life, and one who meant so much to me and to others as well.

CHAPTER 14

Celebrating the Champion of All Champions

CANNOT COMPLETE THIS BOOK without giving you an opportunity to meet the Champion of all champions—Jesus Christ, my Lord and Savior—the One who has intervened in my life numerous times.

Romans 10:9-11 NLT says:

> "If you openly declare that Jesus is Lord and believe in your heart that God raised him from the dead, you will be saved. For it is by believing in your heart that you are made right with God, and it is by openly declaring your faith that you are saved... Anyone who trusts in him [Jesus Christ] **will never be disgraced.**"

If you want this Champion to lead, direct, provide, and protect your life, pray this simple prayer with me aloud right now:

Father God, I do believe that Jesus Christ is Your Son and that He went to the cross to pay for sin, sickness and disease, poverty and lack [spiritually and naturally], grief and sorrow, and spiritual death. When I accept Him as my Savior and Lord, I accept the total inheritance package that He has provided for me.

In exchange for the sin and mess in my life, upon repentance for my sins and acceptance of Jesus as Lord and Savior, I freely receive:

- *Forgiveness.*
- *Healing and wholeness.*
- *Prosperity and well-being of spirit, soul [which includes the mind, will, and emotions], body, finances, relationships, and reputation.*
- *An infusion of His nature, which will mature within me as I spend time in His Word, in prayer, and in developing my relationship with Him; i.e., love, joy, peace, longsuffering, kindness, goodness, faithfulness, gentleness, and self-control.*
- *Protection.*
- *A God-ordained destiny.*
- *Anointing and ability.*
- *Eternal life.*

I am truly sorry for my sin, and I turn from it now and accept You, Jesus, as my personal Savior and Lord. Thank You for empowering me with Your Holy Spirit, who will lead and guide me into all truth. I accept Your Word as the highest standard of truth for every area of my life, Lord.

Thank You for new life in You today, Lord Jesus. I am now a new creation in You. With Your help, it is my goal to grow up spiritually and emanate You in every aspect of my life, Lord Jesus. I love You!

Thank You, Lord, that in this new life, You are a shield around me, my glory and the One who holds my head high. (Psalm 3:3 NLT.) *Amen.*

Postscript

P LEASE PRAY THIS PRAYER over your own life, and add to it as the Holy Spirit leads you. Let love flow from your heart to God's heart, and receive His love back to you:

Father, in the name of Jesus, I declare this to be a new day in my life. You have put Your resurrection life in me, not just to survive, but to live an overcoming, victorious life. You have put me on this planet at this time to live for You and others, not to selfishly live just for "me"!

Thank You, Lord Jesus, for healing my broken heart and restoring what the enemy meant for evil in the premature death of my loved one. I refuse to allow him to destroy or disrupt the anointing You have placed upon my life. Thank You for restoring any physical, emotional, financial, and relationship challenges because of the premature homegoing of my loved one.

I know that my loved one is with You, Father. He/she is not lost! And although he/she has crossed "home base" and arrived in heaven early, he/she is whole, healed, and restored! I rejoice in You, Father God, for Your eternal love and care for my loved one, Jerry Paul (insert your loved one's name) in Jesus' name.

I have said my "temporary" good-bye to my loved one, but as I seek You daily, Lord, You will enable me to "rev up" in the assignment You have given me and complete it in excellence. Then, the day will come when I will have the opportunity to say face-to-face, "Good morning, Lord," and then, "Good morning, Jerry Paul" (name your loved one/s).

God's beautiful promise to you and me from Revelation 21:4-5: No more tears, no more death or sorrow, crying or pain.

"And God will wipe away every tear from their eyes; there shall be no more death, nor sorrow, nor crying. There shall be no more pain, for the former things have passed away.

"Then He who sat on the throne said, 'Behold, I make all things new.'"

About the Author

MARILYN BEGAN HER CAREER as a teacher-coordinator of an Executive Secretary Program at a Community College in Iowa. She holds both a B.A. Degree and a M.A. Degree from the University of Northern Iowa.

After moving to Oklahoma in 1979, Marilyn was employed by Victory Christian Center, Tulsa, for twenty-eight years. First, she taught in Victory Christian School, then edited for the late Pastor Billy Joe Daugherty.

Today, as a senior, Marilyn continues in her God-ordained assignment as a freelance editor of Christian books. Her goal is to make the love and life of Jesus come alive on the printed page.

Vision for This Publication

To help prepare you
to live in a
healthy, wholesome atmosphere
in the earth until the
fulfillment of your days
has come.

To help prepare you
for the New Jerusalem,
your permanent residence!

**"For there is no permanent city
for us here on earth;
we are looking for the city
which is to come."**

—Hebrews 13:14
Today's English Version

* 9 7 8 1 9 3 8 0 2 1 4 7 3 *